CW01512516

Original title:

Zesty Quips Under the Witch Hoof

Author: Daisy Dewi

ISBN HARDBACK: 978-1-80562-982-5

ISBN PAPERBACK: 978-1-80564-503-0

Witty Enchantment from Spider Silk Tales

In the weave of twilight's thread,
Whispers dance where shadows tread.
A spider spins with clever grace,
Enticing dreams in silken lace.

With every twist, a tale unfolds,
Of wizards wise and laughter bold.
A flick of wand, a knowing grin,
Enchantment sparks as friendships begin.

Through moonlit paths, the magic flows,
In every heart, a secret glows.
We wander 'neath the starry dome,
In spider silk, we find our home.

The banter flows, a jovial feast,
In veins of mirth, we find our beast.
Witty words like charms they fly,
Chasing doubts and shades awry.

So heed the tales that nature spun,
With laughter, life has just begun.
In woven threads of joy and jest,
In every heart, we build our nest.

Spunky Sagas Beneath the Witchery Canopy

Beneath the branches, shadows sway,
Where mischief brews by night and day.
A cackle echoes through the trees,
Flaunting tricks on the gentle breeze.

With spunk and sass, the spirits dance,
Each swirl a spell, a daring chance.
A flick of green, a bubble pop,
In sisterhood, the laughter won't stop.

Windswept promises, the night does weave,
Of bravery plucked from hearts that believe.
In whispers shared, a silent pact,
With shadows, we seldom shall lose track.

Frogs and fireflies join the fun,
Under the gaze of the watchful moon.
In every pulse, the forest hums,
With stories of bravery yet to come.

So raise a toast to all who dare,
In the witchery, magic fills the air.
With spunky tales beneath the glade,
Together, our legends are made.

Folly and Fun in Witchcraft's Embrace

In the shadows, laughter gleams,
Cauldrons bubble with whimsical dreams.
Broomsticks dance on moonlit nights,
While jesters craft their silly flights.

Wands entwined in jovial tricks,
Potion splashes bring playful licks.
Spellbound laughter fills the air,
As magic spins in a vibrant flare.

Folly weaves through enchanted glades,
Where every mishap joy cascades.
Charmed giggles echo through the trees,
Brushing against the playful breeze.

In shimmering cloaks, they prance and play,
Chasing shadows that dart away.
Witching hours hum with delight,
As whimsical tales take their flight.

So join the revel, embrace the night,
In witchcraft's realm, pure delight.
For every folly, a memory spun,
In the heart of magic, we find our fun.

Haunting Humor Amidst the Graveyard Roots

In a graveyard where shadows creep,
Ghostly figures begin to leap.
With a wink and a spectral grin,
They drag the living into the din.

Headstones chuckle, whispers play,
As ghouls recount their silly fray.
From cobwebbed trees, laughter weaves,
In the moonlight, mischief achieves.

Coffins rattling in rhythmic cheer,
Echoes of jesters draw us near.
With each haunting, a giggle hides,
Among the graves where hilarity abides.

Skulls adorned with jester hats,
Mock the silence where the night bat flits.
Laughter lingers amidst the stones,
As spirits dance on ancient bones.

In this realm where shadows play,
Laughter feels like a soft bouquet.
So let us gather, spirits sway,
For haunting humor brightens the gray.

Mischief in the Cauldron's Whirl

Stirring chaos in a bubbling stew,
With a pinch of folly and laughter, too.
Cauldrons whirl with secrets untold,
As mischievous whispers begin to unfold.

A dash of giggles, a splash of cheer,
Ingredients conjured from far and near.
Bubbling laughter fills the night,
As potions brew with sheer delight.

Bubbling over with playful tricks,
In this realm of enchanting kicks.
Pumpkins chuckle, and owls hoot,
While wizards jive in a playful boot.

Mischief stirs as wands are cast,
In cauldron's magic, shadows dance fast.
Through swirling vapors, joy breaks free,
As laughter blooms like wild sweet pea.

So grab a spoon, join in the fun,
For under the moon, mischief's begun.
In every swirl, a secret lies,
In the cauldron's whirl, our laughter flies.

Spelled Laughter Beneath the Starlit Canopy

Underneath the starlit sky,
Where dreams take wing and spirits fly.
Laughter echoes through the night,
As magic twinkles, pure and bright.

Wands waved high in playful jest,
In every spell, we're truly blessed.
Whispered secrets float like dust,
In this realm of joy and trust.

Pixies giggle, fairies twirl,
Spinning tales in a soft, warm whirl.
Moonbeams dance on bubbling streams,
As we chase away our quiet dreams.

Laughter sparked by a flickered wand,
Crafting memories, soft and fond.
In the starlight, together we play,
Spelled laughter guiding our way.

So join the night, let your heart fly,
Beneath the canopy, spirits sigh.
For in each chuckle, magic waits,
In layered joys, we celebrate.

Banter Beneath the Broomstick

In shadowed corners, whispers sing,
A broomstick flits on a silvery wing.
Laughter dances in the cool night air,
A spell of joy, if you dare to dare.

With every swoosh, the tales grow bold,
Of wizards young and witches old.
They spin their fables, light as mist,
In hearts entwined, none can resist.

The moon above, a watchful eye,
Winks at the pranks that flutter by.
In the hush between the stars,
Lies magic found in laughter's jars.

So gather 'round, both kin and friend,
Where every jest will never end.
The broomstick sways, as spirits rise,
In banter bright beneath the skies.

With every chuckle, a spell casts true,
Bright as the dawn, and fresh as dew.
For in this realm where shadows play,
The joy of jest is here to stay.

Jests in the Moonlit Glade

Beneath the trees, where secrets dwell,
Laughter rings like a shimmering bell.
The moonlight bathes the ground in gold,
Tales of old in whispers told.

Sprites and fae with twinkling plays,
Join the jest in the glowing rays.
In every giggle, magic swirls,
A dance of joy through leafy whirls.

Jests unfold like petals bright,
In the hush, the world feels light.
Each playful nudge, a spell of cheer,
Turns the mundane into the dear.

With every flicker of the wand,
Imagination wanders beyond.
A dreamscape weaves, the night extends,
In moonlit glades, where laughter bends.

So gather closely, let spirits soar,
For in this realm, hearts seek for more.
With every jest and twinkling glance,
In moonlit glades, we find our dance.

Whimsical Whispers of the Enchanted Night

In night's embrace, where shadows weave,
Whispers float like autumn leaves.
Each secret sigh, a magic spun,
In the quiet, dreams are won.

Stars twinkle low, a watchful crew,
As wishes dance, both bright and true.
A flicker here, a shimmer there,
In this enchanted night, we share.

Through tangled roots and silver streams,
The world blossoms with unseen dreams.
Casts of laughter lift the gloom,
In twilight's heart, flowers bloom.

With every twirl, the night unfolds,
Tales of daring, daring bold.
In whispers soft, the magic's cast,
A spell of joy that forever lasts.

So linger, dear hearts, in this delight,
With whimsical whispers, hold on tight.
For in this realm where wonders ignite,
The night unravels, pure and bright.

Cackles and Cavorts of the Cursed

In twisted woods, where shadows play,
Cackles echo at close of day.
A dance of mischief, spellbound once,
The cursed cavort with glee and dunce.

With every leap, a story's spun,
Of fortunes lost and battles won.
Witches and wizards, bold and spry,
In this moonlit jest, we laugh and fly.

So gather round, for the night is young,
Where every mischief once was sung.
The shadows swirl, a merry chase,
In twilight's grip, we find our place.

Through whispers dark and cackling loud,
The cursed embrace their earthen shroud.
For in the folly, lies the spark,
Of tales that shine, even in the dark.

So heed the call of the trickster's way,
In cackles and cavorts, we lose our sway.
In haunting laughter, the night endears,
The cursed find joy beneath the fears.

Witty Whispers Beneath the Broomstick

In shadows deep, the secrets bloom,
With laughter soft, dispelling gloom.
A broomstick's flight, a whispered jest,
In hidden realms, we jest and rest.

The air is thick with playful lore,
Where mischief waits behind each door.
A flick of wands, and sparks take flight,
We dance with shadows, hearts alight.

The owls, they wink with knowing eyes,
In twilight's grip, the silence lies.
Yet with each chuckle, spirits rise,
For here's a world where laughter flies.

With every twist of wand and fate,
We conjure joy, we celebrate.
Amidst the trees, the giggles swell,
In moonlit nights, we weave our spell.

So gather 'round, both young and old,
Your hearts be brave, your minds be bold.
For in the night, beneath the gleam,
We whisper tales that spark a dream.

Enchanted Banter in the Twilight Glade

In twilight's glow, our voices lift,
With glimmers bright, we share our gift.
A banter sweet beneath the stars,
Where fireflies dance and laughter jars.

We tease the night with playful quips,
As stardust drips from friendly lips.
Each chuckle weaves a magic thread,
Binding friendship, softly spread.

The foliage sways, the whispers call,
In every nook, we find our small.
With wands in hand, we paint the air,
A tapestry of joy and care.

The moon hangs low, a watchful eye,
While shadows flicker, spirits fly.
In every jest, a story blooms,
A harmony that gently looms.

So linger here, in glade enchanted,
With hearts aglow, our words implanted.
For in this space, where laughter's spun,
We find a bond that can't be undone.

Cackles and Sarcasm from the Broom

Above the world on trusty brooms,
We cackle loud, dispelling glooms.
With sarcasm sharp as winter's bite,
We ride the winds, a wondrous sight.

In circles high, we twist and lean,
Our laughter dances, wild and keen.
Each poke and prod, a playful jab,
A merry heart, no room for drab.

The clouds our pillows, the stars our guides,
With every flight, our joy collides.
We streak through night with glee profound,
Leaving whispers of mirth all around.

As spells are cast, and giggles flow,
In broomstick realms, our thoughts do grow.
With every jest, the world we sway,
In cheeky grace, we laugh and play.

So join us now, in aerial jest,
With cackles loud, we are the best!
For in this sky, the rules are few,
We'll soar through night, just me and you.

Moonlit Mirths and Magic Chuckles

Beneath the moon, we leap and twirl,
In moments bright where dreams unfurl.
Each chuckle rings, a spell to weave,
In midnight's charm, we all believe.

The night is rich with magic's grace,
In every twinkling starry space.
We share our tales, both old and new,
With every laugh, our spirits grew.

The firelight flickers, shadows play,
In every ember, memories stay.
With mirths of old and laughter bold,
Our hearts are warm against the cold.

As wands are waved, enchantments sigh,
In moonlit dances, we learn to fly.
With joy unbound, we touch the sky,
In magic's laughter, we shall tie.

So join the night, embrace the fun,
With every giggle, we have won.
For in this realm, where dreamers roam,
We find our joy, together home.

Gales of Glee in the Witching Hour

In shadowed woods where whispers play,
The moonlight dances, casting sway.
Gales of glee in midnight's thrall,
Echoes soft, enchanting all.

With wand in hand, we spin a spell,
In laughter's grip, all sorrows quell.
The owls hoot, the crickets sing,
As magic swirls on whispered wing.

Each flicker bright, a secret shared,
In glistening light, our hearts are bared.
We twirl and laugh, in threads of fate,
Underneath the stars, we celebrate.

For witches bold and friendships true,
In cackling joy, we all renew.
The night is ours, with mirth and cheer,
In gales of glee, we draw you near.

So, come with us, leave cares behind,
In witching hour, let your heart unwind.
The magic lingers, never done,
We'll weave our dreams 'til rising sun.

Quirky Rhymes in the Coven's Den

In a cozy nook, where cauldrons bubble,
Quirky rhymes burst forth from trouble.
With toads and frogs, we share our lore,
Each line a spell, forevermore.

A tickling breeze through windows howls,
In the coven den, we dance like owls.
With giggling charms, we stir our tea,
Each sip a secret, wild and free.

From potions brewed with laughter loud,
To riddles wrapped in a swirling cloud.
The moonlight glints on faces bright,
As rhymes take flight on magic's night.

So gather 'round, dear friends so dear,
With quirky laughs, there's naught to fear.
In the heart of night, we find our way,
In coven's den, where joy will sway.

With every word, our spirits lift,
In quirky rhymes, we find our gift.
So let us sing, with voices clear,
In this warm den, we shed our fear.

Leftover Laughter at the Crossroads

At midnight's gate, the crossroads gleam,
Leftover laughter marks our dream.
With every step, a story lingers,
As fate dances on nimble fingers.

A flickering lantern, a wayward spark,
Where shadows meet in the cloaked dark.
With echoes of giggles, the past unrolls,
In the spun tales, we find our souls.

The laughter rings through timeless air,
In the heart of the night, with joy to share.
We whisper secrets to the breeze,
With leftover laughter, we feel at ease.

Each step we take, a bond we weave,
In crossing paths, we dare believe.
So gather close, dear friends anew,
In the crossroads' charm, our spirits woo.

With twinkling eyes and hearts aglow,
Leftover laughter guides us so.
Through night's embrace, we will traverse,
Where every chuckle is a universe.

Charms and Chuckles by the Full Moon

Underneath the full moon's grace,
Charms and chuckles light the space.
With gleaming eyes, we toss a rhyme,
In moonlit antics, we spend our time.

The whispering winds carry our cheer,
As joyful spirits draw us near.
With dances bold and voices bright,
We celebrate under silvery light.

Each wand we wave ignites delight,
In laughter's song, we take our flight.
Through playful twists and twinkling spells,
In this enchanted night, our magic dwells.

With cauldron bubbling, potions in hand,
We toast to joy, a merry band.
With every giggle, our hearts entwine,
In the moon's soft glow, we brightly shine.

So come along, let worries flee,
By the full moon, we'll roam so free.
With charms and chuckles, we'll dance till dawn,
In this world of magic, we are reborn.

Eccentric Jingles Beyond the Starlit Grove

In the grove where shadows dance,
Whispers twirl in moonlit trance.
Jingles echo, bright and clear,
With every heart, they draw near.

Sprightly sprites with glistening eyes,
Paint the night with gleeful sighs.
Crickets chirp their rhythmic song,
Here in magic, we belong.

Branches weave a tapestry,
Of eccentricity so free.
Laughing leaves, they sway and spin,
Drawing secrets from within.

Twinkling stars in velvet skies,
Guide the wanderers who rise.
They seek treasures lost in dreams,
Amongst the silvered moonbeams.

Time drips like honey on a day,
In this vivid, wondrous play.
The grove hums with joy divine,
Where the hearts and spirits shine.

Revelry with the Rascally Witches

Gather round, ye friends and kin,
For the rascally witches begin.
With a cackle, they weave their spells,
In the twilight, laughter swells.

Brooms aloft, they take to flight,
Chasing shadows in the night.
Potions brew in bubbling cauldrons,
Whispers of secrets, their hidden orders.

They dance with glee through fields of thyme,
With each incantation, they climb.
Stars collide in a cosmic cheer,
As mischief lingers ever near.

In a cauldron of dreams and fun,
Witty banter has just begun.
Toasts are raised to friendship bold,
In this realm where joy unfolds.

With moonlit wands and gentle charms,
They conjure magic, love disarms.
A revelry that never fades,
In the company of grateful glades.

Laughter in the Lair of the Lurking Shadows

In shadows deep, where secrets lie,
Laughter echoes, a joyful cry.
Creatures peek with gleaming eyes,
From hidden nooks, beneath the skies.

Ghostly figures weave and twirl,
As starlit whispers softly swirl.
Comfort found in eerie lights,
Where every fear takes wing and fights.

Through the lair, a spirit plays,
In the echo of gentle praise.
Joy springs forth from lurking gloom,
Chasing darkness from the room.

Cackles ripple like a stream,
Inspiration born from dream.
Here, the laughter finds its home,
In hearts that were meant to roam.

Fearless souls laugh in delight,
Transforming shadows into light.
In the lair, where glimmers glow,
Beneath the surface, joy will flow.

Enigmatic Elixirs of Joyful Fables

In the heart of the ancient woods,
Elixirs flow like shifting moods.
Bottled tales in colors bright,
Whisper secrets of the night.

From berries plucked with gentle grace,
To potions mixed in a sacred space.
They ignite the heart's forgotten fire,
Fables wrapped in pure desire.

Tales of laughter, shadows danced,
Every bottle, a dream enhanced.
Sip the stories, sip the light,
Travel far beyond the night.

Through forests thick, and rivers deep,
With every draught, the memories creep.
Time is woven in every sip,
Joyful fables in each trip.

So raise a cup to tales untold,
In enigmatic cheer, be bold.
For in these elixirs, one can see,
The timeless dance of memory.

Jive with the Jinxed

In a world where wands do weave,
Jinxed creatures dance and leave,
With laughter echoing through the trees,
They twirl and spin with boisterous ease.

Potions bubble, colors bright,
Mistakes made under moonlit night,
With every twist and playful shout,
A swirl of magic casts about.

Beware the charm that goes awry,
For errant luck can fly and die,
Yet joy remains in every chance,
As the jinxed join the merry dance.

In a flurry of sparkles, mischief reigns,
With playful hearts that bear no chains,
The jive continues, swirls and twirls,
Through mystical woods where laughter swirls.

So join the jinxed, let spirits rise,
In the realm where euphoria lies,
With every step, a spell is cast,
For jive with the jinxed, hold fast, hold fast!

Mischief with a Side of Magic

In a corner where shadows gleam,
Mischief brews like a waking dream,
With spells and tricks, they intertwine,
A laugh escapes, oh, how divine!

A flick of wrist, a wink, a nod,
Wand in hand, the world feels odd,
With every giggle, secrets bloom,
As magic paints the darkest gloom.

Through whispered words, enchantments flow,
Unruly spirits steal the show,
Chasing chaos in the air,
With cheeky grins and wild flair.

In capers bold beneath the moon,
A riddle here, a tune attune,
Frolics dance on the edge of fate,
Where every moment's a stroke of great.

So raise a toast to this delight,
With mischief twinkling through the night,
For magic finds its truest form,
In laughter's arms, we all transform.

Tantalizing Tatterdemalion Tricks

With ragged charms and twinkling eyes,
Tatterdemalion tricks arise,
In pockets deep with secrets curled,
A game begins, a wondrous world.

From knotted strings to jumbled spells,
Each whispered word, a tale compels,
With every flick, the chaos sings,
As jumbled magic spreads its wings.

A sprinkle here, a shimmer there,
In every laugh resides a dare,
Through tangled paths of sorcery,
The mischief dances wild and free.

With nimble fingers, cunning grace,
They turn the ordinary into space,
Where wonders twist and mysteries play,
In tangled tricks that sway and sway.

So gather 'round, and do not shy,
Let tatterdemalion spirits fly,
For in their dance, enchantments play,
With tantalizing flair at close of day!

Shadows of Laughter in the Cauldron's Glow

Underneath the bubbling brew,
Shadows dance, and laughter grew,
In the cauldron's warm embrace,
Where joy and mischief intertwine in space.

With flickering light and whispered spells,
Echoes of laughter, secrets tell,
As potion's glow ignites the air,
Creating magic beyond compare.

Through smoky trails of mystic hue,
Laughter trickles, sweet and true,
An alchemist's playful, jolly tease,
With every chuckle, the heart's at ease.

Hidden within the shimmer bright,
The shadows curl and take their flight,
In the cauldron, there lies a quest,
To find the joy that feels the best.

So pour the laughter, let it flow,
In the cauldron's glow, let magic grow,
For shadows twinkling, spirits sing,
In laughter's warmth, the heart takes wing!

Enchanting Jest from the Magic Tree

In the heart of the woods, where whispers play,
A tree stands tall, casting charms in the day.
Its branches dance, with laughter galore,
Each leaf a jest, a whimsical lore.

The breeze carries secrets, sweet and light,
As it tickles the bark, in the soft twilight.
Little creatures gather, beneath its embrace,
To share in the joy, in this magical space.

Bright colors twirl, in a mystical breeze,
Fairies and sprites do as they please.
With flickering wands, they brighten the night,
Crafting enchantments, a wondrous sight.

The moon peeks in, through branches it weaves,
Bathing the laughter in silvery leaves.
Together they frolic, in harmony's song,
In a realm where jesters and magic belong.

As dawn breaks gentle, the jest now retreats,
The tree stands silent, where laughter once beats.
Yet within its roots, the joy holds fast,
A memory cherished, a spell that will last.

Jive of the Jester Underneath a Fallen Star

Beneath a sky, where wishes ignite,
A jester prances, with pure delight.
His cap bells jingling, as he leaps and spins,
A dance of mischief, where the fun begins.

A fallen star lays soft on the ground,
Glistening bright, a treasure profound.
With a twirl and a wink, he sings to the night,
Mirth dances freely, a whimsical sight.

The villagers gather, in awe they commend,
As the jester's laughter weaves joy without end.
His antics enchant, 'neath the cosmic gaze,
Igniting their hearts in a starlit blaze.

Through echoes of giggles, the night softly glows,
With every jest shared, the magic just grows.
And as dawn approaches, with colors so bright,
The jester takes flight, a flame in the night.

Yet, when he leaves, the memories stay,
Of joy and of laughter in sweet ballet.
For a heart that is light, beneath stars aglow,
Holds the power of laughter, forever to flow.

Lively Chatter of the Clever Sorceress

In a tower high, where the breezes weave,
A sorceress dwells, with magics to achieve.
Her cauldron bubbles, casting spells anew,
Lively chatter bubbles, as her thoughts break through.

With potion and herb, she crafts with grace,
Enchantments that twinkle, a dance in their place.
Wisdom flows freely, like rivers of light,
As secrets unfurl, in the stillness of night.

Her mirror reflects, the worlds yet unseen,
With visions of wonders, where fairies convene.
A flick of her wrist, and the shadows take flight,
Chasing their tails in a laughter-filled sight.

The owls hear her whispers, wise and profound,
As spells twist and twine, weaving magic around.
Her laughter rings clear, like a silvery bell,
In a realm where enchantments are woven so well.

When morning draws near, her charms softly fade,
Yet her vibrant spirit in hearts is remade.
For all who encounter her lively charms,
Leave with a smile, and the warmth of her arms.

Humorous Shadows Beneath the Creeping Vines

In a garden lush, where shadows play tricks,
Creeping vines twist, with their silvery licks.
They whisper of stories, both silly and grand,
In the flicker of twilight, they dance hand in hand.

A gnome perched nearby, with a grin on his face,
Joins in the laughter, at a leisurely pace.
His stories of goblins, all mischief and fun,
Bring smiles to the hearts of everyone.

Beneath the green canopy, creatures bestow,
Their jokes and their jests, in the soft twilight glow.
With each little chuckle, the shadows grow wide,
As humor ignites, and the fears they subside.

The moon witnesses joy, as the vines intertwine,
Filling the air with a magical line.
For laughter is woven like ivy so tight,
Creating connections in the deepest of night.

As dawn tiptoes softly, the giggles hold still,
In the whispers of shadows, they echo the thrill.
A garden of laughter, where shadows take form,
Leaves the world lighter, as the new day is born.

Tales of Wit from the Witch's Hovel

In a hovel where shadows dance,
A witch spins tales with a knowing glance.
With a flick of her wrist and a wink so sly,
She whispers secrets that make owls sigh.

Her cauldron bubbles, a potion in brew,
Mixing folly with wisdom, a curious stew.
Cackles of laughter mix with the night,
As she conjures up spells in the dim candlelight.

A cat by the hearth, purring with grace,
Knows all the secrets of this mystic place.
With a twitch of her nose and a swish of her gown,
The tales of her charm spread all over town.

The moonlit sky bears witness so still,
To stories of mischief and magical thrill.
In rhymes and whispers, her legends fly,
Each word like a star in the velvet sky.

So heed well the stories spun in her home,
For in every shadow, a spirit may roam.
With a twinkle of mischief and wisdom profound,
In the witch's hovel, true magic is found.

Spells and Snickers in the Night Air

Under the cover of twilight so deep,
Whispers of magic begin to creep.
With sprigs of thyme and a chill in the air,
A spell is concocted without a care.

Giggling fairies flit past the trees,
Stirring up trouble with mischievous ease.
Cauldrons are bubbling, laughter resounds,
In the heart of the night, where enchantment abounds.

Riddles of magic like shadows do dance,
Beneath the starlit sky, all in a trance.
With every murmur, the echoes ignite,
Casting spells beneath the silver light.

In every corner, a giggle prevails,
As secrets are shared in the moonlit trails.
No need for alarm, it's all in good fun,
For magic and laughter are never outdone.

So come, gather round, let the stories unfold,
Of spells and snickers and adventures untold.
In the night air, where time seems to pause,
Whispers of wonder are the only cause.

Eclectic Echoes in the Forest of Folly

In the heart of the forest, where oddities dwell,
Echoes of laughter cast a whimsical spell.
With creatures of legend and colors so bright,
The Forest of Folly reveals its delight.

Mischief abounds where wildflowers grow,
And stories of folly swirl to and fro.
A twist of the path, a turn of the leaves,
Leads to the magic where no one believes.

Under the boughs of the ancient oak tree,
The echoes of voices sing wild and free.
Each rustle and whisper, each playful shout,
A reminder that folly is what life's about.

With creatures that dance and shadows that play,
They spin the old tales in a curious way.
In the glimmer of dusk, their laughter takes flight,
Each echo a promise of joy in the night.

So wander with wonder, let your heart roam,
In the Forest of Folly, you'll always feel home.
Embrace all the quirks, the peculiar sights,
For magic is woven in the wildest nights.

Frolics and Folklore of the Bewitched

In a realm where the bewitched come out to play,
Frolics of laughter shape the night and the day.
With tales of the curious, the strange, and the bold,
The folklore of magic begins to unfold.

Goblins and sprites in a whimsical race,
Dart through the trees with a glimmering grace.
With mischief afoot and secrets to share,
The night is alive with enchantment and flair.

Around the warm fire, old stories are spun,
Of witches and wizards and spells just begun.
Each flickering flame breathes life to the lore,
As memories gather like leaves at the door.

In the depth of the night, when the stars take their place,
Dreams wander freely with laughter to chase.
And every soft murmur of magic in bloom,
A frolic of joy in the darkened room.

So join in the revels, let your spirit bewitch,
For folklore and frolics are truly a rich.
In the heart of the night, where wonders abound,
The magic of tales will forever surround.

Ravishing Riddles from the Night's Embrace

In the hush of the night, secrets weave,
Glimmers of magic, the heart will believe.
Silvery whispers dance on the breeze,
Riddles unfurl like the softest leaves.

With shadows that twirl in a curious game,
Each flicker of starlight calls out a name.
Mirthful enchantments float through the dark,
Cloaked in the veil where the dreams leave a mark.

The owls in the trees hoot tales of the wise,
Unlocking the mysteries hidden in skies.
With every soft sigh of the night's embrace,
We ponder the riddles that time cannot trace.

Night's velvet cloak drapes the wonders near,
A tapestry woven with laughter and fear.
As ages drift past, the answers will gleam,
Within every riddle lies hope, lies a dream.

So linger a moment, in shadows observe,
Each riddle embraced, each question you serve.
For in every mystery, life's beauty will show,
In the night's tender arms, let your spirit grow.

Chortles of the Moonlit Mages

Under the moon, the mages convene,
Echoes of laughter, a delightful scene.
With potions in hand and wands held up high,
They dance through the dusk, casting spells in the sky.

Chortles resound in the silver-lit glades,
As light-hearted banter flows through the shades.
Infusing the night with enchantments of cheer,
Their giggles ignite, drawing magic near.

The moon watches closely, its glow strong and bright,
As the mages concoct their spells of delight.
With each twirl and twist under shadows they swirl,
Crafting fortunes and fates, in a jubilant whirl.

They hustle and bustle, their laughter rings free,
Creating a symphony only they can see.
With mischief afoot, they share tales so grand,
Of adventures and wonders from realms close at hand.

So heed their sweet chortles beneath the night sky,
For in every giggle, a new dream can fly.
The moonlit mages, with joy in their hearts,
Spin tales of the cosmos, where magic imparts.

Gleeful Gabs in the Shadowy Nook

In the shadowy nook where enchantments reside,
Bright glances exchange, as the secrets collide.
With each gleeful gab, a friendship is sewn,
In the corners of twilight, no one feels alone.

The whispers are soft like the hush of the trees,
Filling the air with a sense of unease.
But laughter erupts, and worries grow small,
As shadows embrace and the night starts to call.

Gather round closer, let stories take flight,
Each tale spun anew under soft starlit light.
From fables of old to dreams yet to chase,
In the heart of the nook, you will find your place.

With each gleeful gab, new legends will rise,
In the hush of the night, beneath twinkling skies.
Bonds twisted in laughter, like vines intertwined,
Create a mosaic of dreams, intertwined.

So venture with courage, your heart open wide,
In the shadowy nook, let your spirit reside.
For in cheerful exchanges, magic takes root,
And the friendships we forge, forever bear fruit.

Silvery Snickers by the Cauldron's Edge

By the cauldron's edge, with a flick and a swirl,
The witches share secrets, excitement unfurl.
With silvery snickers and spells yet to blend,
They brew up distractions, both mischief and mend.

A cauldron of woes, they fill with delight,
With bubbles that shimmer, reflecting the light.
As laughter erupts like the potion's wild dance,
A twinkle of mischief, a nebulous chance.

The night air is charged with the stories they weave,
As shadows croon softly, and time starts to leave.
Each splash of the potion ignites a new jest,
In the glow of the hearth, they are truly blessed.

With every soft cackle and nod of the head,
Ideas take flight, like the hopes that they've bred.
In the heart of the night, where whispers align,
The magic flows freely, like sweet aged wine.

So raise up your goblet, let laughter resound,
In the warmth of the cauldron where joy can be found.
In silvery snickers, the night's spirit glows,
Creating a potion that only love knows.

Jovial Jiving at the Witching Circle

Under the moon, the witches sway,
With laughter bright, they dance and play.
Brooms a-twirling, spells take flight,
In the circle, all feels right.

Charmed air swirls with echoes of cheer,
Whispers shared that only they hear.
Mixing potions, a sprightly brew,
Bathed in hues of silver blue.

Giggling goblins peek from the trees,
Join the rhythm, feel the breeze.
Each toadstool sparkles, a joyous sign,
Where mischief lurks and stars align.

Fires crackle with stories old,
Of daring deeds and treasures bold.
In joyful jiving, hearts unite,
At this witching hour, pure delight.

So if you wander through woods at night,
Listen close, for it's a wondrous sight.
A jovial gathering, a grand affair,
Magic and laughter fill the air.

Giggling Secrets from the Charmed Brook

By the brook, the giggles flow,
Secrets whispered, soft and low.
Rippling laughter, water's song,
Drawn to the magic, all along.

Sunlight dances on silver streams,
Where nature weaves its whispered dreams.
A splash of joy, a playful tease,
Captured moments on the breeze.

Tiny fairies flit and glide,
With teasing grins, they scamper wide.
In this haven, worries fade,
Joyous secrets in sunlight laid.

Every pebble tells its tale,
Of enchanted love and winds that sail.
Giggling echoes, a soothing sound,
In the heart of magic, joy is found.

So come and listen, lend your ear,
To the brook that holds our laughter dear.
In its flow, life's secrets bloom,
With giggling whispers, dispelling gloom.

Folklore of Fun in Witching Stories

Gather 'round for tales of yore,
Where witches tread on ancient floor.
Each story wrapped in charm and grace,
With laughter twinkling on every face.

Whimsical creatures, a playful lot,
In folklore's weave, they tie the knot.
A mischief-maker, a ghostly friend,
Every legend, a twist to send.

From cauldrons bubbling, spells arise,
Mixing fun beneath starry skies.
Witty banter, a magical blend,
In stories spun, the fun won't end.

Tales of potions, wings, and flight,
Of valiant hearts that shine so bright.
In this lore, we find our place,
Where joy and wonder interlace.

So hold them dear, these tales of glee,
In every word, a spark to see.
Folklore dances, a magical play,
Bringing laughter to night and day.

Offbeat Laughs from the Bewitched Path

Along the path where shadows creep,
Offbeat laughs in secrets keep.
With every step, a tale unfolds,
Of whims and wonders, ancient holds.

Gnarled trees grin with crooked glee,
Guarding laughter for you and me.
Mischief curls like wisps of mist,
In this domain, joy can't be missed.

Giggling rabbits in moonlight prance,
Inviting all to join their dance.
With every rustle, fun ignites,
In a world where whimsy delights.

Beneath starlit skies, secrets twine,
With offbeat humor, all will shine.
Every twig and pebble gleams,
In the night, where laughter beams.

So take a stroll, let go of care,
On the bewitched path, laughter's rare.
With every twist, and turn, and laugh,
Discover magic in this enchanted half.

Humor in the Haze of Enchantment

In a world where giggles dance around,
Wands playfully flick, mischief unbound.
Pixies chuckle, in shadows they hide,
Crafting their jokes with sprightly pride.

A wizard once slipped on a banana peel,
His laughter erupted, a joyous squeal.
The cauldron bubbled with bubbling cheer,
As jesters capered, bringing good near.

Broomsticks twirled with a glint of delight,
Chasing the rainbows that colored the night.
Each spell cast with a touch of mirth,
In this enchanted, whimsical earth.

With dragonflies laughing, they swirl and fly,
In the mist of enchantment, their spirits high.
Every corner echoes with joyful sound,
In the haze of magic, humor is found.

So let every heart be light and free,
In this enchanted realm, join in the spree.
For laughter is magic, a gift we share,
In every hidden nook, everywhere.

Laughs that Echo in the Hollow Woods

In the hollow woods where shadows play,
Laughter bubbles like the sun's first ray.
Squirrels giggle, as they leap and dart,
Filling the forest with joyous heart.

Trees sway gently, whispering glee,
In their branches, the world seems so free.
Each blossom chuckles, the breeze joins in,
Together they spin a delightful din.

Beneath the moonlight, fairies take flight,
Sprinkling their giggles like stars at night.
Echoes of joy dance along the glade,
A tapestry woven, a merry parade.

The brook babbles soft, its secrets untold,
Tickling the feet of the brave and bold.
Mirth weaves its spell through the winding paths,
Drawing the wanderers into hearty laughs.

Come, gather 'round the grand old oak,
Listen for laughter, and share a joke.
In these hollow woods, where joy never fades,
Echoing echoes of playful cascades.

Joking Spells in the Midnight Mist

In the midnight mist, where shadows teem,
Wizards gather, brewing their dream.
Jokes like potions swirl in the air,
Each word a spell, crafted with care.

With a flick of a wand, the laughter ignites,
Mixing the moonlight with mirth-filled delights.
Ghosts join in, their giggles resound,
In this mystic realm, pure joy abounds.

A unicorn prances, its mane intertwined,
With ribbons of laughter, enchanted and blind.
The mist embraces each joke that is shared,
With every punchline, the night feels repaired.

Owl's wisdom takes form in a jest,
Witty remarks put every mind to the test.
From pumpkin to cauldron, the night comes alive,
In a haze of laughter, we joyfully thrive.

So venture forth when the mist is spun,
Join the jesters in their merry run.
For in this twilight, where magic persists,
The world finds its heart in joking twists.

Cracking Jokes by the Witch's Hearth

By the witch's hearth, where embers dance,
Laughter entwines with an ancient romance.
Teapots whistle and shadows sway,
As stories unfold in a whimsical way.

The cauldron bubbles with spices and cheer,
With every good joke, more friends gather near.
Herbs and giggles stir in the brew,
Enchanting the night, in every hue.

A toad croaks a pun, as frogs leap about,
Filling the room with a boisterous shout.
Each potion ponders, a chuckle inside,
Echoes of merriment, no need to hide.

Candles flicker, casting warmth and light,
As they share their laughter deep into the night.
The moon grins down, a curious guest,
Listening to jesters, at evenings' best.

So come, sit down, by the crackling fire,
Share a tale or two, possibly conspire.
For by the witch's hearth, humor reigns most,
In the warmth of laughter, we all get engrossed.

Mischievous Mirth Amidst the Potion Parties

In cauldrons bubbling bright and green,
With old wood wands where magic's seen.
Laughter fills the starlit sky,
While gossamer fairies flit and fly.

A sprinkle here, a dash of that,
Turn the ordinary to titters and chat.
The moonlight dances on potion's sheen,
Making otherwise mundane seem like a dream.

Whispers of secrets in air so sweet,
As jests and giggles find their beat.
A riddle tossed like autumn leaves,
Where revelers weave enchanting thieves.

Hidden behind shadows, chortles rise,
From mischievous sparks dancing in disguise.
With flick of a wand and a cheeky grin,
The potion party dances, let the fun begin!

In corners, where treachery often plays,
Sweetened by mischief, in myriad ways.
With twinkling eyes and hearts so bold,
The tales of their laughter shall never grow old.

Snickering Spirits at the Witch's Gathering

By the flicker of candlelit glow,
Gathered spirits, both high and low.
With giggles that echo, a mischievous chant,
As shadows entwine in a ghostly dance.

Old tales are spun in whispered tones,
Of eerie places, haunted bones.
With every chuckle, the night unfolds,
A gathering of secrets, and laughter retold.

The night, a canvas of luminous glee,
Where fun takes flight, wild and free.
In the enchanted woods with endless mirth,
Every heart beats to the rhythm of Earth.

A potion served with a side of jest,
Spirits embrace their ghostly quest.
With echoes of laughter that weave through trees,
The air thick with magic, a cool autumn breeze.

As dusk turns to dawn, the laughter remains,
Forever entwined in whimsical chains.
A snicker, a giggle—the spirit's own song,
At the witch's gathering, where all belong.

Crafty Quips in the Fairy Glade

In hidden nooks where fairies dwell,
Mirth and magic weave their spell.
With tittering tongues and gleaming eyes,
Crafty quips fill the evening skies.

Around the stones where moonbeams play,
Whispers of wonders dance all day.
As laughter flutters on silken wings,
Charming the world with the joy it brings.

Underneath petals, soft and bright,
The fairies giggle, take flight in the night.
With wit as sharp as a thorny rose,
Amidst the glade, their laughter flows.

Every joke spins a tapestry rare,
Flitting about with captivating flair.
A sprinkle of mischief, a dash of grace,
In their crafty words, joy finds its place.

Through leafy canopies, softly they hum,
While stories of old merge with playful fun.
In the fairy glade, where dreams intermingle,
The heart finds its home, and spirits tingle.

Lighthearted Legends of the Witch's Roost

In a nook of the woods, where shadows play,
Legends are told at the end of the day.
With cackles of witches and sparks in the air,
The stories unfold with a whimsical flair.

Gathered round with brews caressed,
Each tale infused with a playful jest.
From spells gone wrong to potions too bright,
Even the moon beams in pure delight.

In this cozy nest of enchanted dreams,
Reality swirls with laughter in streams.
Lighthearted whimsies, shared with a grin,
Where tales of the wild make mischief begin.

Whispers of magic fill every heart,
As giggles echo—never to part.
From the bushes, a chuckle, the wild witches boast,
In the laughter of legends, they revel the most.

So gather ye round, embrace every word,
In the witch's roost, laughter is heard.
Savor the stories, let spirits rejoice,
In lighthearted legends, we find our voice.

Witty Whispers of Cackling Shadows

In the hush of twilight's flight,
Shadows dance with delight.
Their cackles weave through the air,
A tapestry of mischief and flair.

Whispers echo in twisted trees,
Carried soft by the playful breeze.
Secrets known to the wisest wights,
Playing tricks in the moon's soft lights.

With eyes aglow like lanterns bright,
They plot their games through the night.
A riddle spun from laughter's breath,
Tales spun closely, defying death.

Glimmers of mirth in their gleeful snears,
Beneath the cloak of lingering fears.
In shadows' grasp, wisdom does grow,
As laughter flutters, and whispers flow.

So heed the call of the cackling shade,
In their jests, a truth is laid.
For every jest and prank devised,
Speaks of worlds both revered and despised.

Mirthful Comments from the Otherworld

Tales from beyond, where spirits dwell,
In laughter's grip, they weave their spell.
With flickers of light in the darkest night,
They share their wisdom, oh what a sight!

Mirthful comments, like drops of rain,
Laughter dances, washing away pain.
Each jibe a thread in fate's great loom,
Casting joy in the midst of gloom.

From realms unseen, their voices swell,
Echoing laughter, a ghostly bell.
In every chuckle, a tale does gleam,
Painting the shadows, a merry dream.

They nudge and tease, a playful band,
Stirring fortunes with a guiding hand.
For life's a dance, a whimsical game,
In this otherworld, never the same.

So listen close to mirth's gentle sound,
In every corner, enchantments abound.
With every comment and jolly cheer,
The otherworld whispers, "Joy is near!"

Cunning Quips beneath the Cursed Canopy

Beneath the canopy, shadows play,
With cunning quips that lead astray.
Branches twist like a devil's grin,
Whispers beckon, let the games begin.

In this realm where magic hides,
Cursed truths travel like shifting tides.
Every corner, a jest awaits,
Beneath the boughs, mischievous fates.

The owls hoot with cryptic cheer,
Secrets murmur to those who near.
Each word a spark in twilight's glow,
Cunning comments, lessons to sow.

While shadows weave their playful snare,
Dare to laugh and lose your care.
For every quip holds a moment rare,
In the cursed warmth of the midnight air.

Embrace the charm of the unknown,
Letting loose worries that weigh like stone.
For when laughter reigns in enchanted space,
Quips become joy, and fears erase.

Charms and Chortles in the Mystic Forest

In the heart of the forest, where mysteries hum,
Charms and chortles invite you to come.
With every step, enchantments play,
Kisses of magic in every sway.

The trees are alive, with stories to tell,
Laughter mingles where spirits dwell.
A squirrel with secrets, a raven with glee,
Games and giggles, endlessly free.

As sunlight dapples through leaves above,
The forest whispers of wonder and love.
Chortles rise like warm, fragrant air,
Blending moments, casting away care.

In every rustle and faintest sigh,
Lies a charm wrapped in mystery's tie.
So linger a while in this magical place,
Where laughter grows with each tender trace.

For here in the heart of the mystic wood,
Joy blossoms gently, as nature once stood.
With charms and chortles in every breath,
Embrace the enchantment, defying death.

Mirthful Murmurs in the Enchanted Grove

In the heart of the grove, where the shadows play,
Whispers of laughter drift softly away.
Tiny lights flicker, like fireflies bright,
Dancing in chorus, a whimsical sight.

Among ancient oaks, secrets they share,
With each gentle breeze, magic is rare.
The petals unfurl, their colors ablaze,
Nature's own canvas, a wondrous phase.

Squirrels and rabbits, in mischief they thrive,
Chasing each other, so merry and live.
The brook sings a tune, a merry old rhyme,
Echoing laughter, transcending all time.

As moonlight cascades, a soft silver glow,
Illuminates paths where the brave dare to go.
Here dreams are born, and wishes take flight,
In this enchanted grove, where all feels just right.

So come take a stroll, let your worries unwind,
Embrace all the magic, the joy you might find.
For in this sweet realm, where the wild creatures roam,
You'll discover your heart, and perhaps, a new home.

Playful Jests of the Midnight Sorceress

Under the cloak of the midnight sky,
A sorceress twirls, with a glint in her eye.
Her laughter rings out, like a sweet chime bell,
Casting her spells, casting her spells.

With flick of her wand, she conjures delight,
Puppies and kittens, all dancing in flight.
A riddle for those who dare to partake,
Unlocking the joy, with each giggling quake.

As shadows grow long, her magic ensues,
Witty enchantments, she'll gladly amuse.
She stitches together the fabric of night,
Fashioning dreams, in splashes of light.

Now listen closely, to secrets she weaves,
Tales of the stars, and the truth that deceives.
With each playful jest, a lesson is learned,
In depths of dark nights, true wisdom is earned.

So wander the paths, where the moon unveils,
The laughter of sorcery, born of moon sails.
Embrace every jest, feel the thrill of the chase,
With the midnight sorceress, laughter's embrace.

Bewitching Banter in the Witching Hour

At the witching hour, when shadows grow tall,
Whispers of magic beckon and call.
Gather 'round close, as the cauldron brews,
Restless spirits share ancient views.

A tickle of mischief, in every delight,
As lanterns flicker, casting soft light.
The moon grins slyly, a friend to the night,
While the wind curls around, like a cloak held tight.

With potions and charms, they jest and they tease,
Each line a riddle, each laugh sure to please.
Charmed by the moment, with shimmering hair,
Witches weave stories, as light as the air.

They dance upon brooms, twirling with grace,
The strum of a lute keeps their hearts in place.
With every sweet note, mischief unfurls,
In this bewitching hour, magic swirls.

So heed the tales spun in the mystic night,
Where laughter is woven, a tapestry bright.
Join in the revel, let spirits take flight,
In the bewitching banter, hearts feel more light.

Spellbinding Jests on a Cloudy Night

On a cloudy night, where the stars play shy,
A jester appears, with a wink and a sigh.
With cap and with bells, he capers about,
Spreading enchantment, dispelling all doubt.

His words like a potion, peculiar and sweet,
With each merry jest, he stirs up the heat.
Clouds gather round, they listen in glee,
As laughter erupts, wild and free.

With shadows a-dance, he reveals a surprise,
A flick of his wrist, as the moon starts to rise.
He jests with the thunder, he tickles the rain,
All join in the chorus, to banish the pain.

In the murky night air, all worries dissolve,
As spellbinding laughter begins to evolve.
Cloaked in mystery, joy here ignites,
Chasing the darkness, till morning invites.

So gather your friends, let the night come alive,
With jest and with humor, together we thrive.
For in this spellbound embrace of the night,
Magic is found, when the heart is made light.

Delightful Drolleries in the Celestial Night

In the sky, where dreams take flight,
Stars gather, twinkling bright.
Whispers dance on the velvet breeze,
Laughter echoing in the trees.

Moonbeams cast a playful glow,
As shadows sway, they twist and flow.
Creatures chuckle in the dark,
Joining in with nature's spark.

A comet streaks, a wink above,
Shooting stars, tales of love.
Every flicker, a secret shared,
In this night, we are all ensnared.

Hedges hum with secrets vast,
Citadels of dreams amassed.
In delight, the world spins round,
In the night's embrace, we are bound.

So close your eyes, let laughter lead,
In this realm, we plant our seed.
With every chuckle, let hearts ignite,
In the dance of the celestial night.

Enigma and Jest beneath the Ancient Oak

Beneath the oak, where whispers dwell,
Time spins tales, a secret spell.
Leaves rustle with knowing glee,
Guarding jest and mystery.

Curious eyes peer through the night,
Sparks of mischief, pure delight.
An ancient path, where laughter flows,
Crackling sound, each story grows.

With every jest, shadows play,
In this refuge, we're held at bay.
The roots entwined hold truths so rare,
Each giggle caught in the fragrant air.

Around the trunk, the fireflies dance,
Inviting echoes of fate and chance.
Life's riddles spin beneath boughs wide,
Where we shake hands with the unknown side.

Join in the revelry, grow not old,
For mystery's warmth is purest gold.
In this night, with hearts aligned,
We share the secrets, both beautifully blind.

Caustic Chuckles Under Moonlit Glimmers

Under moonlit glimmers, shadows tease,
Caustic chuckles drift with ease.
Witty banter, a verbal duel,
An enchanted night where jesters rule.

The silver light paints tales bizarre,
Each word a spark, a twinkling star.
Glimmers of truth in jest conveyed,
In this twilight, all masks are laid.

With every quip, our voices rise,
In harmony with moonlit skies.
Folly found in laughter's bloom,
Casting away the shadowed gloom.

Figures flit through gardens vast,
Haunting echoes of ages past.
Where whispers cradle timeless schemes,
In the light of our wildest dreams.

So let the night embrace our glee,
As we unravel what's meant to be.
With each jest, let spirits soar,
Under glimmering lights, we ask for more.

Wisecracks from the Emerald Depths

In emerald depths where laughter lies,
Wisecracks bubble, a sweet surprise.
Beneath the ferns, where secrets tread,
Jubilant spirits, nothing ahead.

Rippling streams with echoes clear,
Nature's chorus whispers near.
Each pebble holds a tale untold,
As cheeky jokes unfold, behold!

Among the roots, the past implores,
In every murmur, wisdom pours.
Sassy sprites flit, spread delight,
Making mischief and laughter ignite.

Time stands still in this verdant haven,
Where mirth and insight are freely shaven.
Lose your cares in nature's jest,
In this emerald world, we're truly blessed.

So plant your heart in the emerald ground,
With every chuckle, let joy abound.
In depths profound, let spirits blend,
In laughter's embrace, we find our end.

Jocular Shadows Beneath the Witching Moon

Beneath the moon's enchanting glow,
Shadows dance, a playful show.
Wands are waved with laughter free,
In a world of whimsy's glee.

Goblins giggle in the dark,
Riddles whispered, a spark.
Trees sway with a chuckling breeze,
Mystic tales that tease and please.

Through the glades, the sprites take flight,
Twinkling bright in the soft night.
Chasing dreams, a jolly crew,
Under skies of velvet blue.

Casting spells with just a grin,
Magic drizzles, thick as sin.
Broomsticks twirl in a merry waltz,
No room here for sulking faults.

As laughter echoes, shadows weave,
In the night, we dare believe.
With each cackle, joy doth bloom,
In jocular shadows, lost in plume.

Opening Cackles from the Curved Wand

Wands unbend in twilight's brush,
Incantations spark a rush.
With a flick, and cackle bright,
Magic dances into night.

Curved and clever, spells awake,
Whispered secrets in the quake.
Bubbling potions swirl and sigh,
Beneath the starlit velvet sky.

Hooting owls share tales of cheer,
As bubbling cauldrons draw us near.
Trickster fairies, mischief planned,
In this realm where magic's grand.

Opening laughter, joyous tone,
Chasing shadows, not alone.
Each wave of wand, a charming jest,
In this world where dreams invest.

Cackles echo through the glade,
While frolics of the night parade.
Beneath the stars, we twirl and sway,
In pure delight until the day.

Amusing Adventures in the Mystic Night

Through siren's song and whispered lore,
Adventure calls from every door.
Wands in hand, we brave the dark,
In a quest that leaves its mark.

Pixies dart and shadows creep,
In every corner secrets keep.
Glimmers bright in laughter burst,
Where magic reigns, and fears are cursed.

A riddle spun from moonlight's thread,
Leads the way to where we tread.
With each step, our hearts unfold,
Stories shared, and treasures told.

Enchanting echoes fill the air,
Frolicking with naught a care.
Musty tomes of charm and thrill,
In the night, our spirits fill.

So here's to tales of glee and fright,
In amusing adventures, bold and bright.
As dawn approaches, we'll reminisce,
Of magic woven in moonlit bliss.

Twilight Twinkles of Humorous Spells

Twilight glimmers with teasing fate,
Where jokes and jinxes serenade.
Spells are woven with gentle mirth,
In a cozy world of magic's birth.

Silly snickers fill the air,
As laughter twirls without a care.
Potion bubbles sing a tune,
Dancing light beneath the moon.

Brooms take flight in comic haste,
As wizards prance, no time to waste.
A tickling charm, a gleeful squeal,
In this night, life's a reel.

Goblins grinning, mischief spry,
Chasing shadows as they fly.
Every corner holds a jest,
In humorous spells, we find our rest.

So raise your wand to jesting nights,
Where friendship sparkles, and joy ignites.
With twinkling eyes, we cast our dreams,
In twilight's embrace, nothing's as it seems.

Grinning with the Ghosts of Laughter

In shadows deep where whispers play,
The ghosts of laughter dance and sway.
With glee they weave through misty air,
A tapestry of joy laid bare.

Their chuckles echo, light and clear,
A symphony for all to hear.
They tease the night with spectral glee,
And stir the heart, set laughter free.

With every jest and playful sigh,
The moonlight glints on spirits nigh.
Their glimmering eyes hold secrets bright,
As they cavort through endless night.

A banquet spread of dreams and thrills,
With heartbeats quick and laughter spills.
The echoes weave through time and space,
Where spirits meet with joyous grace.

So join the dance, let laughter reign,
With ghostly friends, free from all pain.
Together bound by joy's sweet thread,
In the twilight where all fears shed.

Raucous Revels on the Edge of Twilight

The twilight beckons, shadows grow,
Where merry hearts and laughter flow.
In raucous revels, spirits sing,
And joy ignites on vibrant wing.

With flickering lanterns, glow and gleam,
They twirl and spin in blissful dream.
A whirlpool of whimsy, wild and bright,
Dancing with stars that pierce the night.

The air is thick with magic's cheer,
As echoes of laughter draw us near.
In every breath, a story told,
Of bonds that form, of hearts made bold.

Oh, feel the pulse of moonlit revels,
Where joy and mischief both sit levels.
The edge of twilight, a sacred place,
Where souls collide in a warm embrace.

So raise a glass to moments shared,
To laughter's light, forever bared.
In twilight's fold, let revels soar,
With raucous joy forevermore.

Quick Wit from the Corner of the Coven

In corners dim where whispers brew,
The coven gathers, wise and true.
With quickened wit and playful charm,
They spin their tales, a magic balm.

Each cackle sharp, each jest a spark,
A flicker of light in the encroaching dark.
With knowing glances and playful jibes,
They weave their spells, each word inscribes.

Around the table, laughter swells,
Each potion brewed, each tale compels.
In shadows deep, where secrets hide,
They share their dreams with hearts open wide.

So gather close, let wisdom fly,
In the corner where laughter's nigh.
With quick wit spun like threads of gold,
The coven's tales, forever bold.

With every jest, a bond that's cast,
In moonlit nights, the die is fast.
In every laugh, a spell is spun,
In quickened wit, the magic's begun.

Tittering Tales from the Twisted Woods

In twisted woods where shadows hide,
The trees whisper secrets, far and wide.
Tittering tales, a capering breeze,
For curious hearts, a fortune to seize.

Each rustling leaf tells stories old,
Of creatures fanciful and bold.
With giggles faint, the phantoms call,
To gather 'round, come one and all.

Beneath the boughs, where magic lies,
The winding paths will mesmerize.
With every turn, a prank unfolds,
As laughter lingers, tales are told.

Through tangled roots and silvery streams,
The laughter mingles with twilight dreams.
A chorus of joy in the night's embrace,
As every shadow finds its place.

So tread with care, and let them see,
The wonders born of jests set free.
In twisted woods, where laughter gleams,
Tittering tales weave through our dreams.

www.ingramcontent.com/pod-product-compliance
Ingram Content Group UK Ltd.
Pitfield, Milton Keynes, MK11 3LW, UK
UKHW021438280125
4335UKWH00035B/292

9 781805 645030